1

The Outcast-You Are No One Till Someone Kills You

Written and Edited by Mlungisi Makhanya

Published by TiwgPublishing

Dedication:

This book is dedicated to those people who try their damndest to live an honest life without fear or favour. Why not? If you gotta die in the name of the truth then, why not….. After all you are nobody until someone kills you…

Prologue:

Happiness is brought by simple things like talk, pat on the shoulder, security, reassurance, a promise for the better life and all such things. Family is the core of happiness for anyone. In Genesis, God created man and seeing that man was lonely, He created a woman to be his companion. This was the first family.

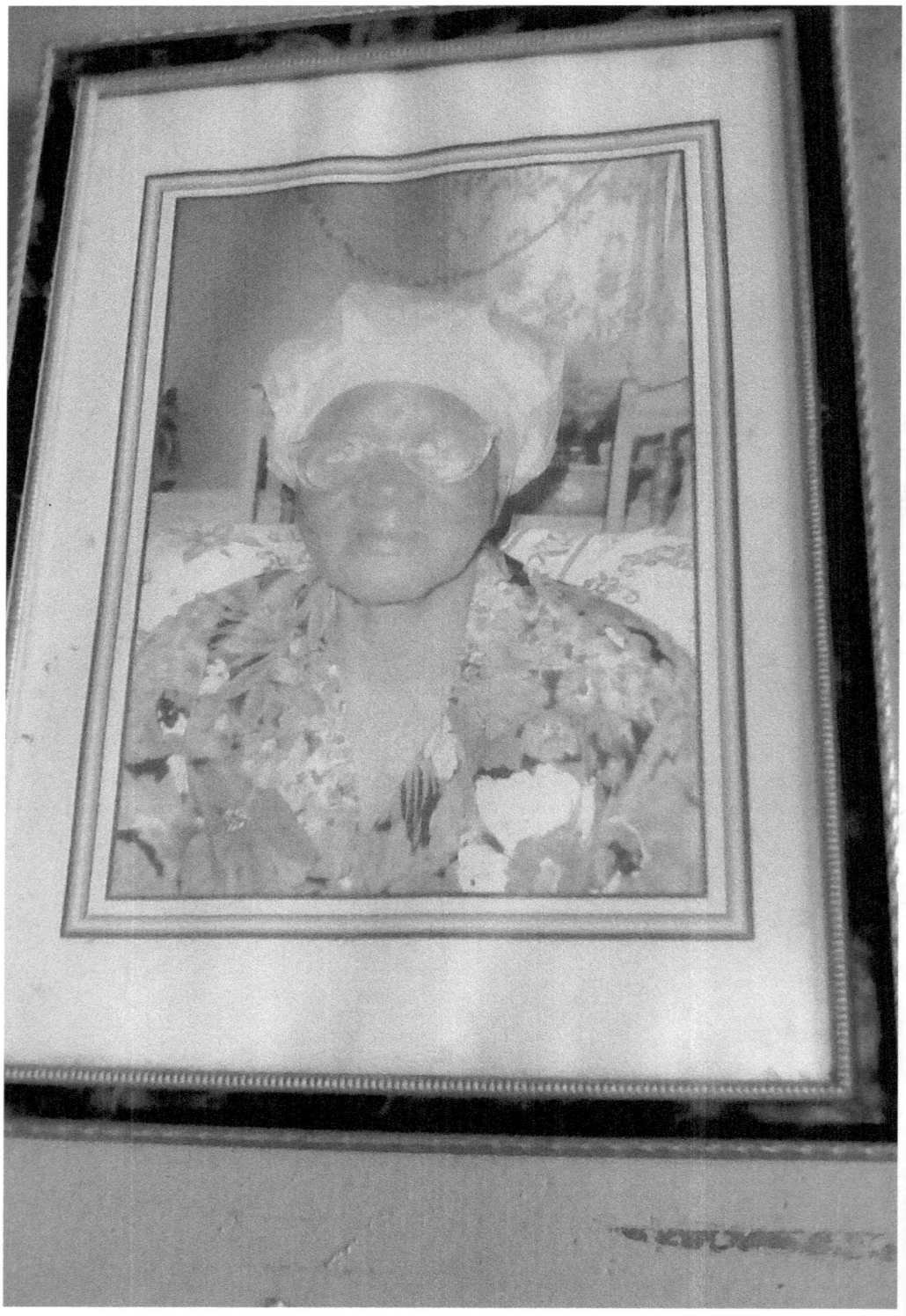

Live and let live

Don't forget that what is poison to me is chocolate to you

Educate to make a living

Create jobs than seeking for jobs

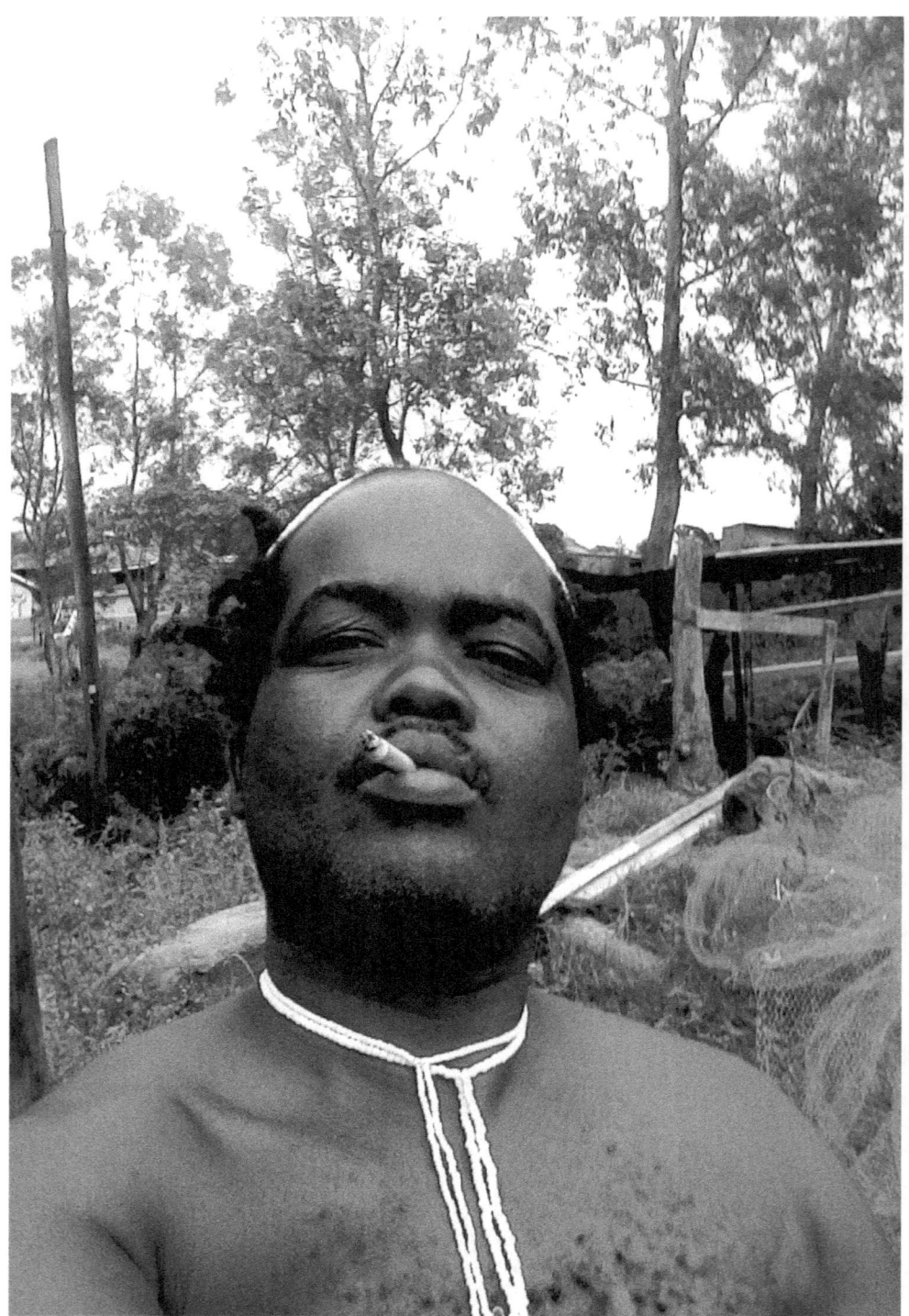

## 1. One Night Stand or Wife?

It was Peeps` first year as a registered teacher. He was appointed to Inhlasana Primary School. Back then schools opened towards the end of January. Peeps had left home to Uthuthwini, a very cool place. It is near the ocean. The specific area he was at was Cool water because of its coolness. It was close to the circuit office. He went there on foot. On the first four days he saw people being appointed to various schools. Finally he was appointed on the Friday of the first week.

He started work on a Monday. It was exciting being in the real situation. He had proven by far that he was going to be a good teacher. On that first Monday all the teachers were going to work. They met with each other at Umzinto; greetings and introductions were made. There were many schools in the area starting on the main road to the inner part of the area called Nyavini. It was so called because a white man used to grow a lot of beans there which in turn was called inyavu nyavu of beans. It meant it was a lot of beans. The white man was called Dick and the area ended up called kwa-Dick.

There were two male teachers who were already teaching in the same school for years excluding the principal. There were also female teachers about four of them in the whole school. All female teachers taught from grade one to grade four and the male teachers taught from grade five to grade seven.

Peeps and one other male were the new teachers in the school. They fitted right in. Both of them lived in the same cottage with two beds for both of them. It was a lonely place to be. It was a life of attending classes during the day, wash your clothes in the afternoon and go to bed thereafter. At least Peeps` room mate had a small radio to which they tuned isiXhosa channel mostly. Peeps loved Nqoloba a news reader who gave an advice that people should eat an apple and not drink.

The same procedure went on for a long time till one Friday Peeps met some local teachers while they all were going to the prayer meeting. Vic was from Lamontville, a very funny guy. His laughter came out of not so much big mustache. He was tall, a drinks` guy who loved friends. He had one problem though, his wife would come and collect him from the friends; like a child he would follow after her while she was holding his hand. It was not cool scene. It was embarrassing even for his friends. She was being disrespective. Vic was friends with Jay, one of those ever laughing people whom you enjoy being with. He was from kwaQoloqolo. He was a homeboy for Slick who was into women from his school. Peeps became friends with these guys.

On that particular Friday I never just met my new friends but something miraculous happened. In the bus therein came 10 women one after the other. I took my time looking at each one of them. There was this one woman who took my eyes. She was light in complexion. She had a round face. As she laughed I melted inside. She was the one my inner voice told me. The funny thing as she came along with the other women I forgot about her. In the bus most teachers drank vodka and I was among them. As the vodka took over my body I began chatting to some women in the bus. They were mostly teachers. Eventually I got to the woman. She was a real beauty, light in complexion, beautifully braided hair and artistically crafted body to die for. I found myself seated close to this beautiful woman with beautiful dimples.

I introduced myself as Peeps to her. She told me she was Happy-girl. I wanted to know where she was going. "I am going home to Umlazi and will return on Sunday." I was glad to have met as I told her. I also told her that I would be dropping at Isipingo and would like to talk to talk to her if she did not mind. She never minded of course. She could not mind, had this attraction to women, it came naturally. This woman was my lady soul. I loved her from the start when I saw her get into the bus. I thought to myself that there was time for us to chat.

\*\*\*\*\*\*\*\*

While Peeps decided to drop us and chose to go with the woman he met in the bus, I and Jay went to the meeting. I was the only new teacher among the old ones. The prayer meeting sat in a hall at Umzinto. We gathered there because we had to pray for the death of teachers in our district. The chairperson of the meeting asked Mr. Z. of our school to come and say an opening prayer. He did the unthinkable. "I have been a teacher for twenty three years and been doing prayers for many years. I want to call Mr. Wishlist to come and do the prayer on my behalf."

I stood up and went to the stage and prayed for the first time in the midst of so many teachers. The meeting went well. Eventually we went home. It was a great experience for me. I have been in the training school for teacher Education, in those 3 years there are not that much chances.

I remember the first year we arrived there. There was going to be a concert for the new comers. Every new student had to come with an act. Peeps, myself and our late friend, Zama did a group dance. Peeps was the leader of the group because he was the one who taught the dance. I must admit that I was a little jealous of that guy. Everything that he touched turned to gold. There were always people around him. He began making money selling cigarettes and continued to do school projects for other students at a cost.

 He was a political leader, giving guidance to others about political situations; holidays as are known today, he used to explain them to us as students. He was good in sports, besides supporting Pirates, he also played softball. He had played almost most sport codes to his exposal in his time.

The chance that I got of praying like that was huge one for me. I will never forget it.

*********

I left home on the afternoon of the Sunday going to my place of work. It was a cool Sunday. I wanted to meet up with Happy-girl. I took a taxi to town and reached the bus stop in time for the bus. I was wearing those big jerseys they called subsidies. In the bus was my new found challenge.  Don't mind me saying she was my new challenge. When we went our separate ways on a Friday we promised to talk on Sunday. I went and sat next to her. She was feeling ok and looking forward to the new week. I was the same as she was.

We talked and got to know one another. She was nothing but a student at Mngomeni High school. She had dropped of High school and started her own salon business. That year she had decided to come back and see if she got her matric. She lied with her father and brother at Umlazi. Her mom stayed alone at Umthalume. Although I was once at Umthalume but I had never been to her side.

 The bus went carrying people at all the stops. Everyone was in the bus, teachers, students and the general public. Those who were not there were latecomers. They would come on Monday.

I noticed where she got off. The bus took us to our school. Finally we went to bed. It was kind of hard communicating. There were no cell phones as much there are at those times. One waited to meet someone. It became a long week for me. What worried me was that I had not prior arrangements for me to meet her.

On a Saturday most teachers were around. We decided to go for a drink in one of the stores. It was after drinking the Smirnoff bottle that we also decided to go and meet teachers from Mngomeni. Jay and his friends were all there having drinks at the pastor`s. e joined in. It was still after two in the afternoon.  They drank till after nine late. The two teachers from my school left me. Jay went to his wife. I was left with Vic and Short. They took me to their women, a commune.

9

I lived with three women at the commune. We cooked separately. My room was a double that I shared with Short`s girlfriend, Mandy. Two other ladies shared another room. Whenever their boyfriends visited I usually was alone with another woman.

That night I was asleep alone as usual. There was a knock at the door. I knew that these were the boy friends of our two friends. My other friend had a boyfriend though he had never come to visit. I became damn afraid to see that they came with the teacher who was hitting on me the past few days. We were listening to the top 20 on radio Zulu. It was how we got our happiness.

Having these three that night gave us some added joy. We danced and enjoyed. I remember still to this day the song we danced to with him. Marvin Gaye, "Let`s get it on" was the song and still is. We danced to the song after he asked me to dance with. The guy was a smooth talker and a dancer as well. I knew I had a boy friend but I also knew that the one in front of me that moment was the one. After we finished dancing I went to sleep. They continued dancing and making happy noise. Eventually everyone went to sleep. Peeps came to my bed. "Take food and eat from the pot then come to bed." I told him. He did as he was told then drink water to clean up his mouth. He took off all of his clothes and mounted himself to the back of my back.

His body was warm against mine but then I shivered at the thought...of having him in my bed. He wrapped his arms around my body. His dick began to get hard. My heart began to beat. He kissed my neck. I moaned slowly and quietly. His hand moved down to my core. He caressed my thighs. I could not resist. I turned and faced him. He kissed me deeply and I was short of breath. His hands were still searching my thighs. They were moving towards my vagina. I touched his dick to have a feel of it in my hand. It was thick and hard. I wanted him inside me. He was in no hurry as he continued to make feel ecstatic. He was cool kissing my breasts; more like sucking them. He moved down my belly button. Suddenly he was licking my core. I never cared whether others heard my moans and screams in the name of love. I was in heaven literally. I loved it. I had never felt anything like it.

Eventually he was on top of me. My thighs were wide open. He pushed his dick straight into my pussy. I felt his dick pushing in and out. He made this unusual movement; like he was stirring a pot making a delicious curry. I loved it. I responded to him making my own moves. Sometimes I could feel myself off the rhythm but got back in it. It was hard at first. It was like we on stage dancing to a song and I never got the beat right. As soon as I got it I heard began to speak in tongues. In a deep voice he called on the Lord, God, and some shouts of Jesus. I could feel he was with me. We were making magic, our magic.

It took us all night to make love. Early in the morning, he left me tired and wondering if and when will he come back to me. He had made an impact-able impression on me. Was it the beginning of something good or a one night stand infatuation?

## 2.  The Vision

Going from Happy-girl`s place to my place was easy. On the way I kept pinching myself. It was not because of sex. It was because I finally had her. I loved her very much. Yes sex was great but it was not the reason why I loved her. It was something I could not describe. If anyone would ask me, "why are you in love with her?" I would just say, "I don`t know." I was simply in love.

I never grew up very close to my father. He was an educative man whom I regarded as strict. Actually there as this thing I loved about him. His love for my mom; they sneaked up every chance they got to be together. It as teenager kind of behavior that made them to want to be together in each other`s arms. Sometimes we would look for them all over only to find that they were in the bathroom. What interested me was the fact that I did not hear the shower running all the while they were there. That reminded me when I still about like 4 or 5 years old. This next door chick would come to my house; knowing that there was no one in the house we would still do it under the bed. It brings the fun in it.

I guess I always knew that there a big Eye out there. It always watches over us all. The night before I had had fun and never thought about anyone in the house. I never thought about hiding the fact I was with her.

The week started. It was work as usual. It was during that week that I saw a vision. A goat in a rope dragged all the way. It led the way. Eventually it came to the final destination. It went into the herd of other goats and disappeared there. Close to me were two men like kneeling down looking after the goats. I greeted the men. Then as I look beside them was a tree. I touched it; it produced milk like liquid that I took and rub on my face. I woke up. I never understood the dream.

Knowing that my family believed in such stuff, I told my parents about it. They encouraged me to get the goat and slaughter it. On a Friday we slaughtered the goat. My grandmamma, rest in peace, was there too.

On Saturday we cooked the goat with dumplings. I had bought some beers and liquor. People were coming from all over. I was stressed somehow. I was restless. My brother Tbose was there. He came with his friends from KwaMakhutha. I knew them and therefore organized something for them.

People called me from side to side. They wanted this, others wanted that! I was taking a lot of strain and I never realized it. Finally I knocked off on the floor and took a very long nap. In that midst I realized that I was no more at home but somewhere else where the gone souls were. There was nothing tangible that I could say I saw.

***************

A friend of mine asked and said, "Tbose, what is happening with your brother, Peeps?" I wanted to spare my brother a lot of drama but I could not. Peeps was seen to be sick. He was having issues inside him. The way I looked at him was like he was in contact with the world we did not know. He behaved abnormally so to speak.

I had noticed that he would go to bed and then he was not even there in the room. Only his body was there. I remember that one night I asked mom to come and watch Peeps while lying on the bed. He was not asleep because his eyes were open. What puzzled me was the fact that he was off it. He was not in the room by spirit. I wondered what went wrong with my brother. I loved the guy. We grew up together. He was older than me and we really mixed in terms of friends but at times we mixed and did things together. When we were young he protected me from other boys. Sometimes he got beaten up because of me.

Peeps went to be sick. His face changed to be oilier. Yes he drank but this was not normal. When he arrived home one time and told us about the woman he had met; we did not believe him. How on earth can someone like him have a girl friend? My mom wanted him to forget about that woman. Her mind never changed even after Peeps had paid lobola for the woman making his intentions known. Peeps had his own mind about the things he did. I truly believed that he was controlled out of this world. He never talked much about the things that happened to him. As a matter of fact, I think we never gave him a chance to show us who he was. The only place you could find what he thought was on a piece of paper. He, the paper and pen were friends. I guess it was his therapy. He became himself in it.

At the end of his first year of starting working he told us that he wanted to go and pay lobola for his wife to be. We were shocked because he had never talked about this woman. Then again it dawned to me that he never actually talked much. I remember organizing a taxi for the family to go and do the job at hand. It was the first I have ever seen, a guy uniting the family through the way of a asking a woman to marry him. People asked friends to do this stuff for them. No, not my brother; he took us all even the smallest of the brothers was there with us. Every member of the family was there. It was a good thing to observe. He was happy, very happy, though he never showed it. I remember his wife was doing a Zulu dance, he never stood up to dance with her, I did it for him. I was proud of my brother.

I was proud of the guy long before. The guy as I have said never talked much but he was seen in action. I saw him conquer women, beautiful women. He was that kind of a man.

What worried me though about him was that though he had this woman by his side, he never stopped being sick. He behaved strangely. When we were all together he would be alone. He never minded being on his own. He lived in solitude. I grew worry inside me. I was never at home all the time but I noticed that he was going through something. It seemed to me that the ritual he did developed into something in. I knew about these things of course. It is in our culture. That is why I took him to see izangoma at Q section, Umlazi.

At the hut of Sangoma, it was said that he was also in line to be one. I knew then that my suspicions were always true about him. I was happy he finally got a solution to his solution. He followed through to what he was told to do. He began to eat izinkamba of ubulawu. My father rest in peace was there by his side through all this. At the end two goats were slaughtered. Peeps and dad wore red skirts {amabhayi} around them and their faces were red from ibovu.

Peeps went about his life and finally got married to his wife two years later.

*********

It was the happiest year of my life. I married the coolest man ever. He treated me the way I loved. A month after our marriage we went and stayed in our own house. It was the first house I could ever called my own. It had three bed rooms. Our family always visited us to see if we were alright. Tbose always checked on his brother. He loved him. I never saw people who though were not together much; but when they met everything else stood. They talked just the two of them.

I remember one night Tbose brought people with him; a lot of men and women and children. Peeps and Tbose talked on the side. Peeps came and let me know what was happening. They wanted a place to stay for December. They were from Port Elizabeth. We had nothing really in the house, a fridge in the kitchen and beds in the bedroom. Our bedroom was respectable. We spent the holidays with them. They were hard working people selling stands they made themselves. Even though we had no food in the house, they covered us. What I never got was where they came to us for the evening. It was a convenience but we managed. My husband got me through everything. He was a patient man. Sometimes I became angry at him for the very soft heart he had.

When we came to live in our first house we had one child our only daughter, Lol. I was pregnant with my second child. Peeps loved her. They connected best than she did with me. I guess being the only child outside the marriage caused some serious damage to me. My husband took his time and loved me but I never had something like that. Not even my own father loved that much. **I guess when a man loves a woman he would do anything to hold on to what he needs.** Lol was going to school. He helped me with everything that had to be done in the house. I loved for him for that.

Sometimes because of the hormones I detested him but he was always there and never minded. I remember when I was giving birth to Lolest; I came all the way from St. Faiths to give birth home. He took me into our bedroom and put on the bed. That day he never went to work. He opened my thighs a little wide and said, "The head is coming out." I was brave even though I say so myself. I was aware of everything that as going on. He went to the kitchen and brought a plastic to which I blew. I don't know how but I followed what he was telling me. I pushed as I was told. The child came out finally. There were then many people from the neighborhood. They took over from Peeps. They cut off the umbilical cord and he came back when I was done.

When Peeps was out he went and brought a friend with him. His name Dave and he was more of a friend to him than the guy who sold him the house. Dave helped us when we bought the house. He helped us pay all the debts. That's how we got the house. He took us to the hospital.

Lolest was not the last child. Mr. T. was born thereafter. He was the handsome of the babies. We never got to stay with him very long. When he was still two months old, close to three months, I took him to church. We arrived home after church late that afternoon; his father took him into his arms and held him while I was cooking. Soon after that there was a heavy storm. It rained heavenly. There was lightening and thunders storm. We all got into one of the bedrooms. Mr. T. was sleeping alone in the main bedroom.

We sang gospel songs. No one of us knew when we went to sleep that night. I woke up very late and went to check on the baby. He never woke up. I was worried because it had been a long time since I fed him. I could not take it any longer and called my husband. I was sitting at the edge of the bed. My husband came and stood at the door way. He took one look at me and said, "He is gone Happy-girl." Not that I did not hear him, no, the message never registered at all. I was still trying to push Mr. T. to feed on my breast when Peeps came and took him. He put him on the bed and observed like searching for some signs in him. I just stood there and watched like I was seeing a movie.

***********

 I sat next to the landline on top of the headboard. I did not know whether to call home or do what. It was as early as half past five in the morning. People were awake; they were preparing to go to their places of work, schools and so forth. Eventually I took courage and phoned my uncle. I told him to tell my mom at home. I hate to be the bearer of bad news and hurt the family, especially. At about eight I called a funeral home. I had an Avbob funeral policy which I had forgotten about. Doves came and took the body. Later I went to them to see what they would need. They gave me quotation of the whole funeral after I had been to the doctor who did the autopsy on the boy. The doctor had told me some disturbing news, "there is no way the child could die from lying on his face on a pillow. Someone must have killed him. I understand that if I write down my findings the insurance will not pay. So, I won`t write down my findings."

At the funeral parlor I let them know about my policy. There was confusion. They sat at ease though saying, "We work closely with Avbob and therefore we will arrange for the boy to be transferred there.

People began to come in at home to check on us. By the end of the week Mr. T. was buried close to his uncle Tbose. Tbose was killed earlier the same year, three months before Mr. T. died.  It was a huge funeral that moved people from all over coming to see a friend buried. Something happened that touched my heart deeply. When it was time for people to come and enjoy food and drinks prepared for them, they went to watch the final between South Africa and Ghana. A few members went home.

Single M. was born a year later being the last member of the family.

Of everything that happened, I was worried about my sickness. I never stopped being sick. There is no type of sickness that I never experienced. It was interfering with my work. I spent more days in hospitals than I did at work. I had forgotten about my vision. I knew that what my brother, Tbose did for me was great. I did appreciate it. I kept having this thing telling me that I never did what I was supposed to do. Getting married was the best thing to happen to me; it was not it. I was not supposed to get married then. I broke all the boundaries. My sickness was a sign. **There was something I had to do about my vision.**

### 3. Things Fall Apart

My wife died first. She was a sick woman. She suffered from severe coughing. I never understood what really was wrong with her. Her illness was taking a heavy toll on her. I was at home that time. I was retired from work and spent most of the time with my wife at home than in the township when I was working. My only boy was at home in the township. He was working at Isipingo.

I tried to take her to the doctor but the medication they gave her did not do anything to help her ease her pain. She continued to suffer right before my eyes.

Our neighbors came to see us bringing about comfort. I was a wreck. I never wanted to disturb my daughter, Happy-girl. She was having her own worries with her husband sick all the time. But, it happened at the end. I had to tell her at the end. My wife died in the early hours of the morning.

I took her to the near funeral home close to our town, Umzinto. It was the worst moment of my life not knowing what to do. I did not have money to pay for the whole thing.

*****************

I knocked off at work like I always did. When I arrived at home there was my mom, Salvado. My wife, Happy-girl was not there. I greeted and sat down. It came straight, "your mother-in-law has passed away." I felt a sharp knife piercing through my heart. I loved that woman. She was more of a friend than just a mother-in-law. I never minded visiting her; just to spend time with her. Her death was rough on me.

I could remember back when we buried my brother, Thabzoro, my mother was very sick. She slept in our daughter`s bedroom next to ours. I believed it was asthma but it was more than that. It was a combination of whooping, wet, whizzing cough that kept her awake all night. It was scary and one stayed on his/her toes because you could not just sleep in her condition. I stayed at night listening to her coughing while I watched the angel next to me. She was quite and slept like a baby. That what happened when she was not worried about anything; that had to do with our marriage. Otherwise she would wake me up at night and talk until she was satisfied. I loved her for it. I thought by speaking we were free of the past events; I should have known better.

I had taken a policy on her life just to make sure that she got buried without any problems. I looked for my policy. It seemed like everything was in order. I asked my mom to hold the fort while I was gone. She had no trouble doing that.

The next morning I went to Umzinto. It was a sad situation there. My father-in-law was depressed. He was hard hit. He was wearing a heavy coat. I had never seen him in that bad way before. He was such an energetic man. He drank his favorite home made vodka to survive. I greeted everyone.

\*\*\*\*\*\*\*\*\*\*

"I am sorry I left you in a lurch. I got the news on Thursday, the day she died. I left the message with mom. I hope she told you everything. My father took mom to Umzinto funeral home. I understand that you have an Avbob Policy. I don`t know if you will do anything about it." She was sad as ever.

"Of course I will go tomorrow when we go to Portshepston Avbob. Don`t worry about it, I will take care of it."

The next day I went with my father-in-law to the funeral home and explained to them the situation and they gave me the price which Avbob took care of.

The funeral was the best. She as buried in a huge casket. D had bought the goat that was needed for the ritual. Everyone was satisfied with everything.

My father-in-law was depressed all weekend. I remember seeing him chat with my father that Saturday. He was beside himself. Even though my father and mom tried to make him feel at ease, it was not easy. He had lost his partner, friend and wife. There was no way of ever seeing her again.

\*\*\*\*\*\*\*\*\*\*\*\*\*\*\*\*\*\*

The death of G. left an empty space to many. To me it brought about my downfall. I know I am saying this because everything bad happened after her death. Actually they were bound to happen. Life at my home was never the same. My illness continued. Even though I did my Management diploma in Education in the two years that followed but I was still sick. I was off school most of the time.

D died a few years after her mother leaving his father alone. I was sick too. I was spending most of the time in various hospitals and somehow I was like neglecting my family.

My wife left me for a long time. She took me to the court for domestic violence. I remember telling the magistrate that I never do things intentionally if ever I do them. Three quarter of my life I do not really know what is happening. I know one thing that I care about my children a lot. I love my wife but sometimes we both manage to bring the worst in each other. Following that I went to the hospital where I was admitted for three months. It was very hard. I ate 24 Pills each time three times a day. I was always tired even in the occupational therapies. I wanted to be free. I wanted to be out of that place. My wife never came to visit me. She had come back home taking my kids from my mom.

When I arrived at work after six months everyone looked at me as though they saw a ghost. I was not about to be intimidated by them. I knew what I wanted to do with my life though I was most of the time out of it. You could say that I was crazy as many people confirmed what they really did not know.

What was happening was that things were falling apart and there was nothing I could do about it. I was told that I was going to lose my wife. I was not about to face up to that fact. I loved her too much. I never saw anything that would separate us. I ignored the voice.

\*\*\*\*\*\*\*\*

My father was becoming ill. He was living all alone after the death of D. I never wanted to be home. I remember he asked me to call my husband and bring him home to him. He asked us to come and stay with him. I hated the idea but I could see my husband was passionate. I thought that he wanted to escape the home bond of our house. He was passionate about my father. He wanted to take care of him. They were more friends more than son and father. He took him to hospital and made sure he got all he needed. I should have loved him more for that but....

I began to develop hatred for him. I hated him for bringing me back to the house I was abused in. I hated him for making me leave my home which was more beautiful than my father`s house. I talked to my friends about it and they all blamed my husband for the same reasons I blamed him for. It was a difficult situation. Seeing him brought nothing but severe hate. I was no more in love with him.

I was advised by friends in light of the fact that my husband was sick; to look out for someone who would take care of me. I was used to all good things. I was more into security than love. I slept in private hospitals. I had a beautiful house in our vicinity. I ate good healthy delicious food. I was losing my husband to illness that I never understood. Sometimes I stayed awake at night and thought "how could I let this happen? My husband had been good to me for a long time; now that he needs me most, I am about to abandon him."

It was done. I don`t think there was any going back. I saw my husband trying hard to fix everything as much as he could but it was too late. I loved him the same way I loved him before. He was a good person, a wonderful and caring husband; he was a good and friendly father. I needed more.

He spent his time with his kids. He taught our daughter how to cook and iron clothes. He stayed with them while I was out gallivanting thinking that happiness was out there.

My father died and we were left all alone. Our house was now looking more decent. My husband had installed electricity, new windows and doors with galvanized burglar guards, ceiling board and cupboards. I was supposed to be more appreciative knowing that he was planning on extending the house but the seed in me was growing. It was a flower growing wild. I hated myself but I deflected it all on him.

I lived at KwaMashu most of the time. I wanted Peeps out of the house. I was hoping to bring my newly found boyfriend home. I never thought what the neighbors would say. I was in love; at least which is what I thought. Was I wrong? Damn God I was very wrong. Man are the same and I found that the hard way. My Peeps was the best man I ever had. I never saw it until we got separated.
I wanted him back but he was gone. He was out of my life.

4. **I Acknowledge death and live anew**

My name is Khululiwe. I live in Cape Town, Khayelitsha. I live to heal people off their indigenous illnesses. This includes performing rituals for those people who are chosen to do this kind of job. I wake up everyday and go to Philippi my place of work. It is hectic. I take a train every morning and return every afternoon to my home. I have met a lot of people in my line of work.

I make medicines and sell them. I require labels for them. Next to my place of work was a man who did that kind of work. I went to see him and he did a good a job for me. When he returned my labels, he talked to me about his plight telling me his vision. I knew what it meant. I was afraid to help him because it would be my first time to do such. So, I told him to go and think it over.

In the following days he came back; he asked me, how much it would take for him to be a complete Sangoma. I told him. He wanted the list of what would be needed to begin. I gave him including the initial fee. We began to spend time together. He was helping me with transport when I wanted to take people for a wash in the forest. He was kind of a shy guy.

One day I took him to the forest for a wash. My boy friend was with us. He helped me wash him. It was the beginning of the long journey. Peeps was a full grown Sangoma by looking at him. He had been living this life for a long time. Though he did not do things fully but he knew in him what was happening. He had a power to see beyond. He talked of things that turned out to be true. His spirits lead him to people who were the same as him. At some stage he insisted on going to Umfuleni at the women's conference. Next door to the venue where he went to ask for water was a woman who had been seeking help for a long time. I was not keen to take her for initiation.

 Things were moving too fast for me. I knew that Peeps had more power than met the eye. In December 2012 we put the official beads on him. Soon after I put the white beads, I began seeing and hearing things. Someone kept saying, "Umndiki nomndawe" and nothing more. I saw Iwisa with red and white beads. I accepted it and said, "Yes I will use it"

\*\*\*\*\*\*\*\*\*

It is amazing how some times a co-incidence happens. The same time I was put on the beads was the time Wishbone passed away. Yes he was my uncle, cousin and friend. He got me. He called me grandpa. At first I thought he was giving me a nickname. As soon as I understood his deep understanding of Izangoma it dawned to me that he meant what he was saying. I was living with Angie`s family at this time. I had spent a lot of money with the ritual that performed on me. I was literally broke. I therefore could not go to his funeral. Besides if I did go it would cost me another close to R5000 to cleanse myself; which is why izangoma do not attend funerals.

I had informed my mom through the phone of my intentions. I still had to come home and do the acknowledgement of death which would give me a new lease on life. Rules had changed for me. There were more things I was not eating. There were things I was not doing. I had to abide by the rules.

I was living a pure life. It was not easy. There was isangoma who was in charge of my beading. He was pompous. I did not like it but I did not care. He became my friend only because I provided transportation to him. I did not mind either. I learnt one or two things from him. He had no wide knowledge and to none comprehension.

My ancestors were becoming stronger. I began to work and made money immediately. Khululiwe took some time out from CAPETOWN. At this point I bought muthi and began mixing. Using muthi names I figured out what muthi did what. I learnt how to group muthi into types.

When Khululiwe was back, we continued to work. The news of my father`s illness never stopped flooding in. I was worried about him. I was also afraid of him. I thought he wanted nothing to do with me. The truth was that on his own he loved me. I wanted to live more years but God has His own plans. He finally passed on.

His death came in time when I was having trouble deciding where to stay. Though Angie`s place was dangerous to live in considering our sleeping arrangement; they were too dependent on me. If I were to do the acknowledgement ritual I had to move out. I was reluctant staying with Khululiwe too. She was too much in love with money. So, with my father passing away; came the opportunity for me to come home.

*********

It was not easy at all but yeah I did. When I and mom bought the land it came with a house. It was small for the family. No one was thinking of extending it. Not that anyone did not care; but everyone had their own commitments and challenges. I was thinking about my ritual and my father`s. And so did others.

My brother was having challenges with his fiancé. He was supposed to get married. This was not the reason why he had come into the life of her bride. This is why they had challenges.

Coming home after my cleansing, I did a ritual called ukujikijela. We still had a four roomed house with an outside toilet. The people began coming home in the morning. We had bought a goat and the sheep. Early that Saturday morning the men went to the bush to hunt as the ritual asks of us. Some men from my family name came early and we all help in cooking the meat. By midday it was all prepared and ready to eat. The sheep was flame grilled. I never ate it because of my situation as isangoma. The day went well.

My main worry was the fact the house was too small for us all living there. I never liked the fact that I sleeping in my parents` bedroom. It was not my main worry! One of my brothers was preparing for his wedding and things were not going the way he had planned. I also wanted to do my acknowledgement of the calling by the ancestors.

I remember one day we were at my older sister`s house because my brother was there whining about his problems in terms of the fact that he was having problems with his future wife; I approached my older sister saying that I had a wish of extending our house but needed someone who can vouch for me at any hardware.

"I have an account that I was hoping we will use at our house but it sees that it will not be happening now. I can use that account to help you. You will pay me of cause."

I don't have a problem my sister as I told you I can afford R2500 a month but after my ritual.

That was our agreement with my sister. There were many meetings in term of the wedding that was to take place in December. In that period my older sister took my idea and presented it as her own. She said she wanted to build us the house. The story was now being talked behind my back. Finally it came to the front and was presented to us all. We began forking in our pockets and funded for the building of the house. The project went well. Everyone who had power to contribute did. It did not matter that I had co-bought the land with mom; I made my contribution towards the house. Towards December it became clear that there was no wedding. The house was almost complete. I was preparing for my ritual. I had no money to do the ritual. I had went from Kzn to Cape town to help my father`s money from his work. It had come. I had hoped it would help. As always other people have their own ideas. My older sister once again made a ruling that the money would further my younger sister`s education; she had a mind of her own too. She had decided to get pregnant and not go to school. That way I was able to use some money to add to what I had to do my ritual after which I paid by contributing more towards the building of the house.

On the thirty first of December I left Durban for Eastern Cape to make sure things was good that side. On that New Years` eve I was with other izangoma singing, dancing, drinking and eating. It was a good experience for me. I was expanding my horizon.

I kept contacting my family through the phone making sure all was in order. This side, things were good. We did ukuphahla. We constantly talked to the ancestors asking for their blessings. I remember on Friday we went to Chancela at a Ndlovu Family Nontsi`s ritual of bringing the ancestors to the home. I met a number of people there.


**********

They call me tamkhulu. I am the head master of our impande. My family name is Ngxabane and so does our Impande. I first met Peeps at a ritual close to Qumbu, a place called Tsolo. I found him to be a respecting mkhwetha. He helped in everything that was done. He was a quite person. Even during the time we spent at Qumbu he would not interfere into adult conversation. He was likeable to izangoma and abakhwetha.

On the day we were going to Durban he was worried about the transport. We had been trying to organize the transportation but things were not very good. We spent hours on the road trying to get hold of someone to transport us. Eventually we got a taxi that took all of us.

We arrived at Peeps` home after seven. They were waiting for us. We did ukutshiza outside the house before we went into the house. Peeps was covered in a blanket as the ritual says. He led into the house. It was a long way from that side to the other side. We entered into the sitting room. Peeps` mom showed us to the room next door. They had prepared it for us to be comfortable in it. There were mattresses around the room. Peeps` aunt came into the room to greet us. She brought a fowl, beer bottles, whiskey, umqombothi, soft drinks to welcome us.

Greetings went on and it was all good. Peeps` family was good and warm. We made a decision as Amagqirha, me, Khululiwe, Zanethongo and uMvangeli to wash Peeps first and so UMvangeli took him to the kraal and washed him. Thereafter Peeps was taken to Indumba. Izincamazane and izimbabhama were brought in and the ritual began. Peeps accepted and acknowledged the existence of the ancestors in him. The ritual continued outside in the kraal. Peeps` mom was very happy. She was taken by us and how we did things.


*******

Indumba is a lonely place to be if your mind is out there where the people are. So, I began ukuphahla and kept my mind on it. I asked for my ancestors to step in to my life. I wanted them to guide me and show me the way I was supposed to take. Not that I did not know it but I wanted to be sure I took the right direction. Back in the day when I first put on intsimbi, I was shown water and someone in red soil and he was red as if he was covered in red mbola. Now I wanted them to clear it all up as to what was happening. I remember that soon as intsimbi was on me, I began to hear the voice, a nagging voice about Umndiki nomndawe but nothing else was said. Naturally I wanted to be clear about those things. I also knew that it was not going to happen instantly, but, I had to know at some stage.

Late that Friday my brother-in-law came. He came straight to Indumba and checked on me. I was wearing in white. We talked a bit. He was coming from work. I asked him to collect my ithwasa sister and her mother. They arrived with two other izangoma. I had reserved a bottle of J&B for them because I knew his grandfather loved it. I was called from the Indumba and went where everyone was. We did ukuxhensa and ukunqula. Photos were taken. At that moment I had no phone to take photos with. I had been given a phone in a vision I had while in Indumba. That meant that I could use the phone.

Something happened that night. Every Sangoma went out flat dead and slept it all like they were kids.


\*\*\*\*\*\*\*\*

I woke up early in the morning. I had enjoyed Imvumakufa of Peeps. He was my first Thwasa and was proud of him. He was a grown Thwasa in terms of idlozi. I and other izangoma were worried about uMvangeli who got lost during the night. We knew that he was into this disappearance thing. At Tsolo he did the same. We did ukuxhensa and ran out in the yard. We did the same routine for a couple of hours.

UMvangeli came that morning. All Amagqirha went out and burnt the bones. All Amathwasa were locked inside the house. They were not allowed outside till the process was done and dusted.

Thereafter we began preparing to go. Tamkhulu called us into Indumba. We had to eat ingcaza. The whole family was there. It was all fun. Peeps' mom drank a lot of whiskey not knowing it was whiskey. Tamkhulu said, "I never saw a bold woman in my life!" That was Peeps aunt. It was a good time for the family to bond. We shared in everything that was there.

Finally me, Zanethongo and Peeps met. Peeps gave us money. I got my fee and Zanethongo got transport money for us all. We said our goodbyes and Peeps accompanied us.

## Chapter 5 –Living Anew

Everyone left me with my family. I was a fully fledged isamgoma but I also knew there was more work to done. I was used to indumba and its procedures. I was not fully aware of some signs, guides and revelations; so, I needed to be constantly in communication with someone knowledgeable.

Talking of signs, one night I went to bed and I could not sleep. I heard this voice nagging me about snuff, so, I went to indumba and put snuff in my noise. Thereafter I was able to sleep. The next morning we were sitting outside enjoying sunshine and fresh air as usual when two women came to my home. They wanted isamgoma. I came to attend to them. In indumba one of them demanded I gave her snuff which I did. She constantly smoked and it dawned to me that the ancestors were telling me that she was coming my way the next day.

I was able to help them with their various problems and they paid me for it.

They were not the last to come. A brother of mine came to me in search of his lost cellphone. Apparently he had lost it because some two girls robbed him while he was drunk. They had worked with two other boys. What happened while he was in indumba was exciting.

I saw his mother crying and holding her hands at the back of her head.

She was somewhere at her husband's old home. I told him to bring his parents to me.

What I told them about my vision was confirmed as she said, "true, my body is hurt and scratched as though at night someone has been beating the hell out of me." It was the last time I saw them. They never came back to see me. His mother never came back even for her monthly prescription.

With me things never stopped. One night I was about to go to sleep when the voice instructed me to sleep in indumba. I did that. I was about to sleep when suddenly it happened.

I was floating in the air looking down onto earth. I saw a black cow eating on a very green grass. There were green trees. Then the voice said, "Look down for a red small tree." I looked but never saw it. "Look carefully" Then I saw it but then it turned into a hole. A tail was going down into the hole and climbed onto it. It took me into the ocean. Again I saw houses. The voice of the same man called me into the house, a round house. I went in and found IGONA. In the next two houses I found the same thing.

As we float above the ocean I collected five sea shells and put them together with Amagona.

This vision made me tell Khululiwe about it. She said something about imfukamo but I realized that it was more of umndawe thing more than anything. I was not worried. I knew they would show me everything. They had told me a few months before in a vision. They were kneeling down with izithebe in front of them. They promised to me everything. I believed them. It was happening. I was in the game.

It was not before long that I was introduced into a group of muthi. My understanding and knowledge grew stronger. I learnt a lot.

Then I met her. She was the woman in my vision. Her face, her knowledge surpassed the knowledge I had seen before. I knew she was to take me further. I began talking to her through whatsapp.
We chatted and I knew she was the one. One day I called her and to my astonishment she had this voice; strongly womanish woman which was very twitty.

\*\*\*\*\*\*\*\*\*\*

Peeps came to my home after sometime of talking. My name is Siyanda from Uitenheige. We hooked up with Peeps on whatsapp and I loved him. I loved the way he explained things to me. I asked him to visit me in order to help me.
He arrived at 12 in the morning after the whole day of travelling. Our local meter taxi driver brought him. There was me and my ex at home. I asked if he wanted to eat but asked for the tea after which he slept.
The next day we woke up. I introduced him to my ex. They were easy to get along. Peeps was a smoker and so did my ex. I joined them too.
At midday my brother who lives in the outside building came in and met Peeps too. They chatted. It was easy to chat to Peeps because he spoke isiXhosa.

The two guys prepared themselves to go to work. We were alone with Peeps. We began fooling around like we did on whatsapp. He kissed me and caressed my body. Finally we made love on the floor. We organized something to drink. We even went to my indumba after cleaning ourselves up. There was something special about Peeps. He had this connection with whoever he was talking too. I must admit I was taken aback by it. I loved him even more. I was worried about my ex though. I knew he came home very late. So, we had all day along with Peeps.

Eventually he left me for Cape Town. He promised me to come back to me before he went to Durban.

Yes we talked although we were apart. After a week we met again. He only stayed for the weekend and left on Sunday. My stay with him was remarkable. He helped me in more ways than one. I owe him the tortoise.

**********

Coming back to Durban from my trip was revitalizing. I found out that one of tamkhulu`s amathwasa was coming to my home for umndawe. She came at nine in the evening. I could not send her away.

I waited till in the morning to hear here story. She told me that her father Q wanted her to come to my home. She was going to be ithwasa for umndawe. I accepted her. We did a few welcoming rituals and sent her home. She had to go home to finish ithongo elimhlophe. Before that we went to her father`s home. I spoke to him telling him that I would take the job. I requested him to guide us on our quest.

www.ingramcontent.com/pod-product-compliance
Lightning Source LLC
Chambersburg PA
CBHW070426190526
45169CB00003B/1424